Disney

102 DALMATIANS

Joke Book

An Afghan hound walked into a pet shop.

'Why the long face?' asked the shopkeeper.

PUFFIN BOOKS

Howlers written by

Dickie Dungworth

Design ruffs by

Fifi Grant

PUFFIN BOOKS

Published by the Penguin Group
Penguin Books Ltd, 27 Wrights Lane, London W8 5TZ, England
Penguin Putnam Inc., 375 Hudson Street, New York, New York 10014, USA
Penguin Books Australia Ltd, Ringwood, Victoria, Australia
Penguin Books Canada Ltd, 10 Alcorn Avenue, Toronto, Ontario, Canada M4V 3B2
Penguin Books (NZ) Ltd, Private Bag 102902, NSMC, Auckland, New Zealand
Penguin Books India (P) Ltd, 11 Community Centre, Panchsheel Park, New Dehli - 110 017, India
Penguin Books (South Africa) (Pty) Ltd, 5 Watkins Street, Denver Ext 4, Johannesburg 2094, South Africa

On the World Wide Web at: www.penguin.com

Penguin Books Ltd, Registered Offices: Harmondsworth, Middlesex, England

Published in Great Britain by Puffin Books 2000

1

Made and printed in England by Clays Ltd, St Ives plc

British Library Cataloguing in Publication Data

A CIP catalogue record for this book is available from the British Library

ISBN 0-141-31071-5

Disney's 102 Dalmatians

Joke Book

PUFFIN BOOKS

Why are Dipper and Domino no good at hide and seek?

Because they're always spotted!

What's black and white and blue?

An unhappy Dalmatian!

What's white with black and red spots?

Dipper with the measles!

What kind of puzzle does Cruella hate most?

Spot the Oddball!

What do you call a tiny Dalmatian?

A micro-dot!

What do you call dancing Dalmatians?

Polka-dots!

What goes DOT-DOT- DOT, DASH-DASH-DASH, DOT-DOT-DOT?

A Dalmatian in a hurry!

How does Oddball get out of so many scrapes?

Because she's always all white!

What do you call a naughty Dalmatian puppy?

A trouble spot!

What do you call a pretty Dalmatian?

A beauty spot!

What's the best game to play with Dalmatians?

Dominoes!

Did you see the newsflash about Cruella's Dalmatian dognap?

It was an on-the-spot report!

Dipper

What do you get if you cross a Dalmatian with a sausage-dog?

A dash-dot-dashhound!

What do you get if you cross a Dalmatian with a kangaroo?

A spotty jumper!

Why are Dalmatians the greatest?

Because they knock the spots off other dogs!

Then there was the reformed Dalmatian, who changed his spots ...

Why didn't Dottie tell her pups the story of the puppy-snatchers?

In case they got carried away!

What's harder to find than a needle in a haystack?

Dipper in a domino factory!

Why does Oddball never need a bath?

Because she's spotless!

What is black and white, has four legs and a trunk?

Dipstick going on holiday!

What happened when Chloe bought Dipstick a lead?

He had a new leash of life!

Dottie

What's the difference between Oddball and a teenager?

Oddball wants to get spots!

What is the latest fashion in Maison LePelt?

Jail wear!

Why can't Alonso, LePelt, Horace and Jasper make good soup?

Because too many crooks spoil the broth!

What does LePelt call his team of models?

The fur brigade.

Where would you find a recipe for Cruella cake?

In a crook book!

What do Cruella DeVil and a pub landlord have in common?

They both spend most of their time behind bars!

What do Cruella and a shepherd have in common?

They both have a crook to help them!

What is Cruella DeVil's motto?

Keep a cruel head.

What would you call a two-foot tall Cruella?

A little DeVil!

ALONSO: I've hosed down the puppies now, mam.

CRUELLA: I said to give them what for, you fool, not wet fur!

Why did Digger refuse to dig for his bone?

He was being bone idle!

What do you call Drooler with a bone in each ear?

Bone deaf!

What do you call Chomp with a banana in each ear?

Anything you like – he can't hear you!

How does Dottie call her friends?

On the tele-bone!

KEVIN: One of my dogs has no nose!

CHLOE: How does he smell?

KEVIN: Awful!

KEVIN: Why is Chomp making that ticking noise?

WADDLESWORTH: He's training to be a watchdog.

Which of Kevin's dogs is best at football?

Drooler, because he dribbles so well!

What is Waddlesworth's postcode?

RUA K92

Little Dipper

Knock! Knock!

WADDLESWORTH: Knock! Knock!

KEVIN: Who's there?

WADDLESWORTH: Macaw.

KEVIN: Macaw who?

WADDLESWORTH: M' cornet's melting - let me in!

Can you only see Dalmatians in certain places?

No, they're spotted all over!

Does Dottie wash herself quickly?

No, she likes to lick her legs, then paws!

KEVIN: Chomp, what are tree trunks covered in?

CHOMP: BARK!

Woof! Bark! Ruff!

KEVIN: Correct! Digger, what goes on top of a house? It's a ...

DIGGER: WOOF!

KEVIN: Well done! Drooler, what do you make from grapes?

DROOLER: WHIN

Ruff! Woof! Bark!

KEVIN: Good boy! Waddlesworth, what's the opposite of smooth?

WADDLESWORTH: RUFF!

KEVIN: That's right!
What a clever bunch!

Domino

ALONSO: I'm sick of LePelt calling me a stupid little man, mam.

CRUELLA: LePelt, tell Alonso you're sorry.

LEPELT: I'm sorry you're a stupid little man!

Why did the staff at the bakery work long hours?

Because they kneaded the dough!

KEVIN: I've just taken in an Alsatian with a fever.

CHLOE: Is that what you call a Germy Shepherd!?

Why is Dipstick's rear end like a tragic life story?

It's a long moving tail!

What's white, has four legs, and can see as well from either end?

Oddball with her eyes shut!

CHLOE: Does Digger wear a sunhat when it's hot?

KEVIN: No, just pants!

KEVIN: Where's Chomp?

WADDLESWORTH: He's just popped out for a bite!

KEVIN: Which side does Dipstick have most spots on?

CHLOE: The outside!

Which fish does Chomp chase?

Catfish!

What's black and white and black and white and black and white?

Dipstick in a revolving door!

Oddball

What's black and white with sixteen wheels?

Domino on rollerskates!

What's Digger's favourite instrument?

The trom-bone!

KEVIN: My sheepdog ate too much jelly yesterday.

CHLOE: What happened?

KEVIN: He got the collie-wobbles!

After the dognapping of several Dalmatian puppies, police are following a number of leads.

CHLOE: What do you use to wash your dogs' fur?

KEVIN: Shampoodle!

ALONSO: Now Cruella is in jail I have a new job as a litter collector.

KEVIN: Have you had training?

ALONSO: No, I'm just picking it up as I go along!

What is Drooler's favourite song?

Drool Britannia!

CUSTOMER: I'd like to buy one of your fur coats, please.

LEPELT: What fur, madam?

CUSTOMER: As little as possible!

What does Cruella call LePelt?

Her Frenchman henchman!

CHLOE: Why do you call your new dog 'Sandwich'?

KEVIN: Because he's half bred!

CHLOE: Which of your dogs is most expensive to look after?

KEVIN: The Deer Hound!

Drooler
Waddlesworth

CHLOE: Why does one of your dogs go 'WOOF WOOF TAKE THAT'?

KEVIN: He's a Boxer!

CHLOE: What about the one who goes 'WOOF WOOF BOING'?

KEVIN: She's a Springer Spaniel!

CHLOE: And the one who goes 'WOOF WOOF HA HA'?

KEVIN: He's a Laff-ghan Hound!

CRUELLA: Alonso, fetch me a fur coat immediately!

ALONSO: What fur, mam?

CRUELLA: I want to wear it, you fool!

Which bark is the hardest to hear?

Tree bark!

KEVIN: Now, Drooler, if you and Digger shared a bone, how much would you have each?

DROOLER: ARF!

KEVIN: Good boy!

ALONSO: What fur do you get from a skunk?

LEPELT: As fur as possible!

What films do Dalmatians like best?

Black and white ones!

Did you hear about the Dalmatian with musical spots?

He made a fur-tune.

JASPER: It's raining cats and Dalmatians out there.

HORACE: Don't you mean 'cats and dogs'?

JASPER: No, it's only spotting!

What do you call a Dalmatian sitting in the sunshine?

A hotspot!

Chloe: Have you seen my big dog bowl?

KEVIN: No, is he any good?

KEVIN: One of our new dogs keeps going BANG!

CHLOE: Perhaps he's a gundog!

KEVIN: Yesterday, I lost one of my golden-haired puppies.

CHLOE: Retriever?

KEVIN: Yes, thanks, I found her in the garden.

LEPELT: Bear fur is exquisite. Have you ever hunted bear?

ALONSO: No, but I've hunted in just my shorts ...

- **What kind of music do Domino, Dipper and Oddball like?**

- Pup music!

If Chomp swallowed Jean-Pierre LePelt, would that be an in-terrier-designer?

Why would Chomp never bite a clown?

Because they taste funny!

Which of Kevin's dogs did he find at the top of a mountain?

The Peke!

Knock! Knock!

Who's There?

Kennel.

Kennel who?

Kennel be calling round later!

What type of trees does Jean-Pierre LePelt like best?

Fur trees!

Why didn't Cruella want to end up in a cake?

She didn't mix well!

What did Alonso say when Oddball escaped?

Dog-gone!

KEVIN: Chomp got fined this afternoon for making too much noise.

CHLOE: A barking ticket? That's ruff justice!

What's black and white and red all over?

An embarrassed Dalmatian!

What's the difference between a coyote, and one of Chomp's dogfleas?

One howls on the prairie, the other prowls on the hairy!

KEVIN: I took Drooler to see a Flea Circus yesterday.

CHLOE: What happened?

KEVIN: He stole the show!

ALONSO: Why does a polar bear have a fur coat?

LEPELT: Because he'd look awful in a mac, you fool!

Which dog is like a raspberry jelly?

A red setter!

CRUELLA: Where did all the fleas go?

ALONSO: Search me.

CRUELLA: I'd rather not!

KEVIN: Oddball slept under a leaky oil tank last night.

CHLOE: What happened?

KEVIN: He woke up oily in the morning!

What's the difference between a horse race and Cruella's collection of overcoats?

One's a few furlongs, the other's a few long furs!

Then there was the time Chloe's dogs caused a stir on holiday. It was a Dalmatian vacation sensation.

What is Jean-Pierre LePelt's favourite kind of dance?

A fur ball!